"Ken Weisner is in awe of the Great Horned Owl—its silent flight, its skill as a hunter, its eerie, deep-throated call—and he addresses every poem in *Songs for the Great Horned* to the owl, and considers him a confidant and mentor, a sentinel who has seen it all. One might imagine that every poem takes place in the forest and in the dark of night, but Weisner's Great Horned has been a witness to history, and his presence in the poet's life is expansive and hardly limited to a region of bosky wilderness. In one poem, Weisner tells the owl, 'You would love Doris Day,' and there are cameos here by Billie Holiday, Benny Goodman, and Harriet Tubman, among others. This is a book about owls, but also about history and family, about art and music, about loss and the consolations of love.

— GARY YOUNG, author of *Even So: New and Selected Poems* and *American Analects*

ℚ

"In *Songs for the Great Horned*, Ken Weisner takes us on an unforgettable spiritual journey, a journey of avian, human, and personal memory. A journey of grief and gratitude. The Great Horned, here, is a stand-in for all of us: resourceful yet vulnerable, loved yet not loved, displaced by unprecedented devastation to habitat, confused by the rapidly changing and often hostile world it once could count on. The vivid evocations, power, and sensitivity of Weisner's poems are transformative, leaving us haunted and humbled, 'time itself, a whisper to protect us, like sleep.'"

— ROSE BLACK, author of *Clearing, Winter Light,* and *Green Field*

"Here is a jewel box of owls! Here is a book of second person owl poems—poems in which the you is a strange shape, a meadow sound, a cypher, a memory, the Maquis, Yahweh, snakes, ghosts, the speaker, a grandbaby, two strangers, death, every mystery, 'time itself.' The yous in this book sing and swoop and hunt. They devour. They mate for life and feed their young. These yous have horns and talons. They outlive even as they flee and hide. 'I see we are you,' the poet writes, and the world in this book is the world I want to live in — strange and dreadful as it is — it still lasts. It has lasted. May it last still. 'I am sometimes in dread of the sharp little binary of truth,' the poet writes inside these pages, 'It cuts and cuts into nothing.'

—LISA ALLEN ORTIZ, author of *Guide to the Exhibit* and two chapbooks: *Turns Out* and *Self Portrait of a Clock*

Songs *for the* Great Horned

Songs *for the* Great Horned

☙

poems by
Ken Weisner

SHANTI ARTS PUBLISHING
BRUNSWICK, MAINE

Songs for the Great Horned

Published by Shanti Arts Publishing

Designed by Shanti Arts Designs

Shanti Arts LLC
193 Hillside Road
Brunswick, Maine 04011
shantiarts.com

Owl woodcut on p. 16 by Grace Brieger and used with her permission; owl image on pp. 5, 15, 29, and 47 / Fernando Cortés / AdobeStock; image on p. 9 is an excerpt from *The Last Judgment* by Lucas Cranach the Elder, 1524; image on p. 30 is *Great Horned Owl*, by Keith Hansen, 2013, from *Birds of Point Reyes*, used with his permission; image on p. 38 is from a bestiary published in England around 1235; image on p. 48 is by John James Audubon and Robert Havell, *Birds of America*, 1827; image on p. 56 is plate 32 in *Urania's Mirror*, a set of celestial cards accompanied by a treatise on astronomy by Jehoshaphat Aspin, 1825, image restored by Adam Cuerden.

Printed in the United States of America

ISBN: 978-1-962082-15-0 (softcover)

Library of Congress Control Number: 2024930921

for Becky

Contents

Acknowledgments

Caesura: "Blues in Slow Swing"

Catamaran: "I Come Across You Sleeping"

Jung Journal: Culture and Psyche: "Cowboy"; "Incident Report"; "Thomas of Monmouth"; and "You Mate for Life"

Phren-Z: "Little Songs for the Great Horned"

☙

Thank you to readers and supporters Charles Atkinson, Rose Black, Grace Brieger, David Denny, Bob Dickerson, Andrew Gent, Keith Hansen, Frances Hatfield, Diana Hartog, Rosie King, Paul Kolhoff, Stephen Kuusisto, Marie Maeda, Lisa Allen Ortiz, Marilyn Patton, Robert Pesich, Sarah Rabkin, Becky Roberts, Joseph Stroud, David Allen Sullivan, Amber Coverdale Sumrall, Matthew and James Weisner, Tom and Stan Weisner, Dana Levy-Wendt, Gary Young, and Christine Cote of Shanti Arts Publishing. Special appreciation of Krystyna Weinstein's *The Owl in Art, Myth, and Legend* (Savitri Books LTD, London,1985) and Scott Rashid's *The Great Horned Owl, An In-Depth Study* (Schiffer Publishing, LTD, Atglen PA., 2015).

I

Incident Report

Tapetum Lucidum

You notice the rustling of a nocturnal mouse thirty millionths of a second later in your left ear than your right. So you adjust-left the periscope of your head. Just a little, accordingly. All light comes to you twice, in the deep layers of the eye. *Tapetum lucidum*. From the Paleocene. You spread talons, raise them in front of your face. You fly like held breath. When it is time, you close your eyes.

"Leading-edge serrations, velvet-like surfaces, the fringes of your trailing edge." The Air Force studies your wings. They study you. You pick a bat from midair. Silence is acuity to get where one intends with no distraction or lost energy. To be suited for motion with no drag. You are breathtaking, precise. I go to the meadow. You dive from the redwood crown, glide the last fifty feet just above the dry grass in the twilight, drop into the weeds, scrabble around, then up to a nearby branch where a fledge shrieks and joins you. I imagine he's getting too old to be fed this way. But you feed him, he demands it. He is at that age — almost an owl, not quite an owl. The awkward adolescent still learning to hoot, to hunt. The meadow is new-mown, early summer, dusk-lit with snakes and rabbits.

Cowboy

A boy rescues you and names you Shane after the gunfighter. *You have been one acquainted with the night.* You have a mysterious past. At dawn, you drink your whiskey—at dusk, the bitter coffee. You choose your words carefully. Your owlets—only half will reach adulthood. It's a tough world, hombre. You are a loner, who was once a provider. There is beauty in it. Like Bach in the organ loft at Leipzig. What you know is beyond words. *The woods are lovely, dark and deep.* The boy loves you because you are fragile and you are Gary Cooper. I love you because you are Robert Frost.

You would love Doris Day. Everyone does. No, you wouldn't. "Is the future that hard to see?" The falcon has a special tooth to finish off prey. You stab rapidly, crush, suffocate, break necks for expediency. Does prey die before you swallow? You have no teeth. Form is our holy mother. She holds all equally and tenderly and says yes to all life. I want to talk to you about aging. There are days I feel half alive, hanging from your mouth. When I had one hundred stitches in my arm, I could not get over their intricate beauty. It takes millions of years to become something else. For the wings to become utterly silent.

Incident Report

You were there at the beginning. You flew under the radar and out of the Mesozoic, out of the age of conifers, into the Paleogene (Cenozoic), past the Neolithic, past Neanderthal, past the Titans, Olympians, Pharoah, past Babylon, past the Phoenicians, right through and in and out of the Promised Land. Past Charlemagne, all the Kings, Popes, Civil Wars, World Wars, Genocide, past collective madness, split atoms, split genes, right to this tree crown, this cold Friday night, Lord have mercy. How do I report what I have seen? Will someone write this? My life has been taken.

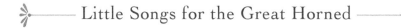

Little Songs for the Great Horned

Winding up Old San José Road
at dusk, I pull into a curve, and
it's as if you have always been
there, ears bent to the ditch from
a low branch. I pass right through,
but you make an impression, as
on gelatin silver, onto my feelings,
latent, permanent. It is the begin-
ning of something.

ॐ

I move to the woods. You call
from atop sixty-million-year-old
forests. You have climbed up
from clay, from the Paleocene.
You cleave like two notes on a
wire, play your mediaeval chant.
One of you coos — feathery, soft —
that's Billie Holiday. The other
lowers the pitch a tone on a hol-
low, woody reed. That's Benny
Goodman. You vibrate duets
from rooftops, car radios, belfries,
clefts in the faces of cliffs.

≈

One fall day, embers the size of unfurled wings. You're not used to being hunted. This sort of migration is not in your bones. Smoky half-night. Santa Ana gusts. You'll end up behind a grocery sign in town, or in a woman's garage behind the clothes dryer. Maybe on your own—toxic smoke, separated from your kin. Where to find food? Nesting by the interstate in a frazzled pine. Scouring ditches along the frontage road, the tracks.

≈

A thousand homes. Felicia's home and studio burnt to the ground. One home torched in Boulder Creek while ten feet away, Charles and Katie's doesn't burn. I offered them our guest room. I can't change the world that much.

❧

It's a trick of the wind, a meadow
replete with you. The firefighters
are winning today. I wish them
good fortune. There's a shooting
star. Crickets set the background
beat, fledglings interject. You call
from the treetops.

❧

Every so often a firefighter finds
a fledgling and rescues it. Do
you know it's burning insanely
ten miles away? Throughout the
West, like never before?

❧

There is no pyro-diversity to re-
turn to. No food source—no food
source for your food source. No
beetles in the ash. No beetle lar-
vae. No understory, no mosaic,

no patchwork with hideouts. No
woodpeckers. No green. May-
be next year, wildflowers, a few
hummingbirds.

CR

Geologically speaking, you've al-
ways hunkered down, taken the
night shift, taken whatever you
could find. A refugee. You're cast
as an outlaw, harassed by mobs.
You've become, over millions of
years, a creature of the night. As-
tonished by disdain, you hone a
quiet dignity, speak a strange and
beautiful language.

CR

Today, you've returned. A theme
and variation, polyphonous, echo-
ic, fugal, imitative, plainsong, an
organ, an instrument. You hear a
twig break under snow.

CR

Your ears are asymmetrical. The right a little higher than the left. Therefore, you place me perfectly in space. You can't fully see but can precisely imagine. Hello, you tilt your head, is that Paul Robeson singing?

CR

A shape that is probably you, a shape that holds steady, perhaps moves slightly—we're not quite sure—and then a shudder, a jolt as wings the size of a man launch without sound across the whole field of vision, then the moon, then the larger dark.

CR

Before sleep, lying side by side, I am sure we are both great horned owls. Ridiculous! Only baby owls sleep lying down. But for that

instant—the blanket of feathers
over our long bodies, wings fold-
ed in—I see we are you.

ଔ

One night, in a near-sleep, win-
dows shut, I hear two of you. So
faint, I count slowly to fifty and
still can't swear it. Same thing be-
fore dawn. Is this really you, or
just my inner owls? You, or just
the memory of you? I am some-
times in dread of the sharp little
binary of truth. It cuts and cuts
into nothing.

ଔ

I love you more than ever, but it
is harder right now. Paul Farmer
died in his sleep in Rwanda. I see
you fly down from the same bare
branch at dusk. I hear you in the
middle of the night.

II

How You Come for Us

Martin of the Southwest Wildlife
Federation of Utah

rescues you from an older couple's yard, your wing broken. When Martin gets there, the older gentleman who called dispatch says, "look at the eyes, will you look at those eyes. Those crazy eyes."

He wants those eyes in his marble collection. Look at those *boulders, bonkers, coshers, mashers, plumpers, poppers, shooters, thumpers, smashers, gooms, noogies, taws, bumbos, bowlers, tronks, hoggers, toebreakers.*

Oh, baby. "Calm down, friend," says Martin.

"Will you look at that creature. Will you look at those peepers!" The man is acting like he found wounded Jesus—or ET, the extraterrestrial. "I never knew we had them here." He and his wife take photos: just Martin and you, then he and Martin and you, then his wife and he and Martin and you. Martin's wife demurs. Martin, a quiet man, has you by the ankles, immobilizing but displaying razor-sharp talons—cradling you like a baby, facing you forward while you lie against his forearm. It's your lucky day—a clean radial break, not a fracture across the span.

Martin has seen you hit by cars, seen you shot—a family thought you were evil. Or caught in leghold traps, tangled in barbed wire, rat poisoned. Electrocuted. Occasionally, a snake, a porcupine. Or you starve. But it's almost always humans.

Yet also humans, maybe six weeks later, like Martin, who release you, two-hand underhand, tossing you to the sky. Creating the world. With a throw that never comes down.

How you hold your ground at the tops of the redwoods while fireworks blast just a street away, the mortars and the bottle rockets. It doesn't faze your gaze over the fresh-mown meadow rustling with moonlight.

Bill Sadler, vet from a few doors down, what it takes for him to get through this night, cocooned in headphones, passed out on the basement couch, his dogs restless. How powerful the hiss, concussion, the refrains.

Your hearing? Ten times as good as a human's yet holding your position in the tree crowns. Then five huge cannons — each followed by a hissing ten-times-higher-than-a-tree-tall chrysanthemum, spray-shower of blood and bubble gum, yellow-gold and lucky-green. All above the street but flickering here like a black-light Saigon disco ball, so bright I can see illuminations of you in movie frame pulses.

But you've had enough.

Your wings strobe-unfold. In each of five lit frames, you take a flight deeper into the woods. Turns out you weren't immune to the pounding strafe of false day.

A little sad to see you go—yet thrilling—to watch you rise—in that surreal light—like watching statuary come to life: the gargoyle flies from the cathedral.

I want to tell you my feelings, share my ideas on military spending. The ones causing war, how often are they the ones most devastated? By losing a family, a village? A wife, a child?

Small comfort: you'll outlast us. You'll be back hunting voles and field mice before the children are tucked in their beds, before the firecracker casings are damp with dew.

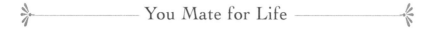

Out on your usual spindly redwood branch suspended like a fishing pole in the August sunset. Above the dry grass. You are a fisherman, hook and line. You are patience, tool, and craft.

You mate for life. Sometimes, rarely, if no chicks, you'll fight. Maybe, after five years, you'll kick him out for good. A serious reason. Something years in the making. Something bigger than either of you.

I heard talons the day I left. Rabbit one minute, meat the next. Carried along into this new home. Dusk dense with stars and the roar of crickets.

There are mouths to feed. Later, invisible, your names on each other's tongues. You sing a step higher; your four calls overlap his five. You are close, you could be anywhere. I hear you from my bed, like memory.

I Come Across You Sleeping

I come across you sleeping midmorning. Across the creek only ten feet up a redwood at the crook of a branch just near the trunk. Neck tucked in. I think I see white facial markings and V-tufts even though you are utterly still, so for the longest time I can't be sure you are there. I want to see you, so have to weigh the possibility that you are a trick of the fancy. Tucked away behind dead branches. Then when I have given up hope of being sure, you move, and it's you—a cat with wings. When you turn later and face away, the feathers of your back camouflage against the redwood bark, and I can see why you chose this place. But roosted facing outward across the creek, your outline is clear, and your mottled, gray-brown head and feathery texture. You preen, fluff. Brown creepers and ground squirrels appear nearby, unafraid in the dappled canyon shade. They somehow know you are resting, sated. Do you guard a nest just out of sight? I sit on the knuckle of a giant root in that intimacy. I don't seem to bother you. So I sit still in my own thoughts as if I have finally found my church, just off a well-used trail; people walk by, dogs come up and sniff. But I am lost in meditation and in you. In a sense, what could be farther away? You are as far away as the stones I set on my father's grave. As if he were under water right here. As if the stones were a world we shared. As if we could touch in the stones.

Hoot-owl calling in the ghosted air,
Five times calling to the hants in the air . . .
Robert Hayden, "Runagate Runagate"

A whole lot going on across just a few bars—stump like an auction block, dark wood like a middle passage. When you call, it's swung, like a Charleston, but think two or three lifetimes before the beat. Pick up the feet. It's Jim Crow. One more time, it's the Great Migration. It's call and response.

My father may be alive. Only the dogs know where he went.

There's swing in the slowest realms. Realm of whale cries and plate tectonics, and ancestors who would have lived full lives had they been so lucky. Realms where time slows down—the Roaring Twenties into the Great Depression; you, the Great Horned, sing, and the other you answers over a patch of land as big as a lifetime, forest acres vast as generations.

Tonight, a freight-whistle slides on by. Swung blues. Many Thousands Gone. They say Harriet Tubman spoke Owl. To keep us alive, she had to know rivers better than anyone, and birds.

I'm sure of it. I was poking around in your pellets last weekend and saw there the exoskeletons of crickets, the fibers of roots and reeds, gopher bones, feathers and bills of a sparrow, teeth of rabbit, claws and fur of a housecat. And the deeper I looked, the closer I came to the destruction of the temple, the humiliation and exile of my grandmother, and there was the skeleton of the Lord, and there, as *in fimo*, the true bone and teeth of William of Norwich, a thorn of his crown, some talons freshly chopped, all like a hagiography, silent, opportunist, a thousand-year shadow.

You, he cannot hear any more than a rabbit. I am speaking of the Eagle-Owl, your ancestor. But he can see your silhouettes across the hills at Carabanchel. This is where Generalísimo Franco will build his famous prison. When the Inquisition grills Goya about *Maja Desnuda*, he escapes with his life—friends in high places. In his seventies, he buys Quinta del Sordo, a crumbling estate. He paints *Saturn Eating His Children* directly onto the wall above the dining table. Saturn! Not faced with starvation but with losing power over others. So he destroys them. The artist is deaf now. From syphilis? Mercury? Lead? In the *sala grandé*, Judith brandishes her nine-inch blade.

This evening you show interest in the French Resistance. Dovid and Regina Knout, Abraham Polonski, Adriana Scriabina ferrying children, Simone Segouin a.k.a. Nicole Minet derailing trains at Chartres, rescuing shot-down airmen, forging papers. Dimitri Amilakhvari, fighting in North Africa, and with just a few men, routing Rommel at Bir Hakeim. Women, Georgians, Armenians, Poles, Catholics, Jews, living the double lives of the tricolor.

"We foreigners, have only one way to prove to France our gratitude: to be killed," Amilakhvari says.

You, *Bubo virginianus*, implacable and undistracted, take in the awful fact of the Vichy Milice. The heroic beauty of the Maquis.

You have lived here for millions of years, maybe sixty million. Once you were double the size you are today; imagine your cries, your moon-lit shadows, your noiseless ten-foot wings.

You continue your examination of the meadow, the forest floor, and any incipient rustling of mice and voles, rabbits, snakes, any meaningful motion scrabbling or scurrying.

You probably think this is an allegory. You are the Jews (perhaps) or you are the Poles or the Maquis. Or you are Yahweh. Or the Jews are the mice, and the Nazis are you. Or the snakes.

I only know which names are in my mouth. The history is written. Ghosts and shadows are my brothers and sisters.

A code, a password, moves between you.

You are surprisingly austere. Visible high above, perched on the end of a bare branch. Straight-backed in your pulpit, staring out over the meadow, motionless against the smoky dusk, you hunt field mice. You clear your throat.

One

Like a gargoyle flying right off the cathedral at evening —
or spilling across the book of life, vines moving gilded past
margins, across the worms of books, you came for my
father. You took him with talons strong as the jaws of an
attack dog. A mighty strike and suffocation.

You're not a smiler. You don't need to be liked. You
watch and feed. You came for my father, and you will
come for me.

You came twice for my mother. Three times for my
grandmother — walked her through the streets pinioned
with a star. Took her husband and her son in the space of a
summer day. Now one eye always checks the sky.

Two

But it was not you that did these things.

I free you from the foolishness of history, from gargoyles, the New Age tarot, the comparisons with archangels. War, religion. And I free you from Athena, Merlin, Aesop, Bosch, Harry Potter, and Carl Jung. Free you from all signs and apparitions, full moons, graveyards, witches, Halloweens and hexes, fears of night, fears of the forest, the number thirteen, devils. Free you from bad luck, good luck, portents of death, shamanic feathers.

Just your gaze, unredeemed.

Free you from guardianship, from curse, from your bones in my soup, from human stories and human souls.

But I cannot free you from beauty, or how you come for us.

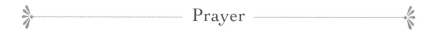

Prayer

Soon I will put on my face. Time itself, a whisper to protect
us, like sleep. That is what you remind me of, that whisper.
To have seen the two of you hunting in the moonlight,
standing among treetops across the meadow is like having
seen a single stitch of another world, darker, the ink of
some living hand, the embroidered iota. Thank you. I saw
none of it.

III

Warm Blooded

Watching the Biggest Game of the Year

You are motionless atop a tree-crown overlooking the house
I lived in for thirty years. Some multi-millionaire bought it,
fixed it up. We are across the street at Dave's. They start
these games at dusk west-coast time for the nationwide
broadcast. Dave has DirecTV. Two screens! My son has
joined us! This Giants/Dodgers match is like Ali/Frazier.
The Thrilla at Pac Bella. The game of the century.

It's the third inning. My son and I open the screendoor.
Across the street is my son's room and the window he used
to sneak out of. Upstairs is the converted attic I gazed
from for decades, dark as a crow. We step outside. In an
alternate universe, we never walk back in. We stay out
long after you fly off, and we walk down by the shore. But
I only imagine this universe in retrospect, after they've lost
one to nothing, the way one might ruminate about any loss.

When I dressed superstitiously for the game, I wore the Neruda shirt over the Gigantes shirt over the swoosh spiral tie-dye, which should tell you or anybody else everything they need to know. Skin, pale and scarred beneath. I brought my lucky glove, but my heart wasn't 100 percent in it. I was already yours.

You were scarce back in 2010. They won the whole thing. I still lived there. It was jays, crows, mockingbirds. The trees did not tower over the roof lines, lawns, loneliness, or gable windows. I was aching to be carried off. By then, the boys were gone. I missed them. We had a little old TV up there. I will tell you, I wept.

Deep forest, evening, early spring—uphill, rounding the switchback. You call nearby, low, maybe twenty-five feet off the ground, visible on a redwood branch. Out to feed more than just yourself. Four calls with the full force of your smaller male body. Between long silences, you speak. Minutes pass. When you take off, you glide so close, then on into the deeper woods below. My mouth forms an "O," draws a full intake of breath, a held lungful of air, and awe.

I'm supposed to be home. Dusk has finished filtering down the woods. I look at the time; there's a message on the phone, from my son. A little child named Bean is in the womb! Well, the size of a bean. They've waited so long. But today the doctor couldn't hear her heart, so they were concerned, even went right away to a specialist to see if Bean was at six weeks or seven weeks. It made a big difference. Most of the day, they thought maybe they'd lost her. Then the second doctor said to wait a while. "She's likely OK in there. She's just not the fetal age we thought she was."

Early next morning, you, the female, are nearest, grand and healthy feathers fluffed. You've come close to call, resonant through your body's instrument, the chill canyon, the smitten labyrinth of the ears. You announce day the way your mate signaled night. The morning's movements overlap, your greeting and farewell among sparrows waking excitedly in misty light. You move outward and away. But also inward through the conch into the imagination. What am I without you?

Just last night, standing only a few feet up the trail, there you were. I reached into a pocket for the phone and called my son. What could I say? Now I have seen you, heard you, twice, a dusk, a dawn. And this morning, I fly through the meadow saying Bean, Bean, Bean, Bean, Bean.

For an hour you call out atop a Norway Spruce. How could you not be freezing? I imagine your full length, feathery gown, and contoured down. A subarctic swim jacket. No moon to witness or warm. Just your puffs of song from among the cold staves of the high branches. Millions of years of music across the boreal.

You survive the cold, down to forty below. Somehow you live, you hunt. It's February, so you incubate, pull the egg against the blood, to your brood patch. For more than a month, you cannot leave the nest for more than twenty minutes or the shell will freeze. Your mate brings back fresh blood from under the snow.

My own granddaughter is growing. She gurgles now and bubbles communiqués in her one-piece sleeper. It is seventy-two degrees inside her nest. She is fed and warm. She is exploring the edges of her body, hands, mouth, crib. She coos like you. She too can sing.

Dear ones, you are right there, fifty feet away, calling out —
and instead we peer right past you at Neowise, a comet
scientists say appears only every 6,800 years. Icy, dusty,
spewing light, ancient as civilization, so the creationists
will say.

We obsess over the light far beyond you that will not pass
here for another 6,800 years, and what will humankind
be then?

How small we are, gobsmacked. Huddled with our
tiny binoculars in the half dark to watch Neowise sail
past at 144,000 miles per hour, yet somehow frozen
motion. We see it with our four eyes and our four arms,
the way we often look at you, but this time, right past,
right through you.

They say when it last flew over 6,800 years ago during the
late Ubaid, it was "a period of increasingly polarized social
stratification and decreasing egalitarianism." I've seen a
glimpse of the pottery at the Louvre.

And the time before when it flew by, it saw something
amazing on the Aleutian bridge — the first human
settlers making their way onto a new continent. So many
undocumented immigrants! Following what star?

Like a doorway it opens, marks a clock, fathoms deep.
How is it possible not to be astonished?

It is exhilarating and quiet when we go in. To have seen the comet! Yet nearly all I can think of now is you, the constant, greater marvel. Marvel of eyes, wings, feathers, neck, ears, claws. You came to us. Marvel I heard tonight but did not fully see.

You aren't to be found straddling the tail of Hydra, Corvus alongside, and Libra. You didn't make Ptolemy's list. I've seen you imagined, drawn by Jamieson. But never codified. Apocrypha, unworthy of even the most minor house of the zodiac. Overheard. Overruled. Outcast. More Egyptian than Greek. Perhaps you make those in charge of the night uncomfortable? Are you glad you're out of there? Just now, did I see what I think I saw? Your shadow? You're so close, each coo like a fixed point on a starless chart, crossing the clearing, your owlet's infancy spared, doted upon, and treasured, the foundation of everything.

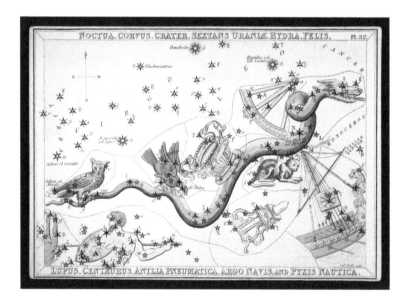

In bird memory, which is precise and effortless, the moon has been known to disappear in the dark before dawn, and return. These astronomers do not know why; they rustle in excitement, won't stop chattering at the glow of eclipse light. It suits them to live in a world of probabilities. There is much to consider.

You great horned call each other home as first chill of waking hits early risers—commuters, insomniacs, monks. A mile down long haulers shift through the straightaway. Mellow buzz, sweet chatter of the very young, a double celebration in the canopy.

Dark, foggy treetops—hard to see anything tonight. But two young people are coming out of the woods. She emerges, looking at her phone. He's a ways behind with the dog and making noises, yips and yowls. "What are you doing?" she asks. "Trying to scare you." She snorts at this.

She stops close by. "Oh, my God, look at that bird," she says. She points over my shoulder. She turns on her phone light. I twist around, look up, and there you are, just twenty feet above. I wonder how long you've been there standing with me in the dark. "Yup, that's a great horned," I say.

They look my way now, a murky form, a shadow. "They're looking for wake-up snacks in the fresh-mown grass," I say. "They hunt rabbits, gophers, snakes."

"Oh, we didn't see you," she says, nervously, shining her light. I turn and watch you fly off. The young man and the dog are quiet now. They are turning to leave. "This is a great place for owl watching," I say.

Sources

[p. 18] "The Meadow"
"Leading-edge serrations, velvet-like surfaces, the fringes of your trailing edge"
Adapted from abstract of this article: "Owl-inspired leading-edge serrations play a crucial role in aerodynamic force production and sound suppression,"
Chen Rao, Teruaki Ikeda, and Toshiyuki Nakata, *Bioinspiration & Biomimetics*, July 4, 2017.
https://pubmed.ncbi.nlm.nih.gov/28675148/Bioinspir Biomim, 2017 Jul 4;12(4):046008

[p. 31] "Martin of the Southwest Wildlife Federation of Utah"
"boulders, bonkers, coshers, mashers, plumpers, poppers, shooters, thumpers, smashers, gooms, noogies, taws, bumbos, bowlers, tronks, hoggers, toebreakers"
Adapted from Wikipedia entry: https://en.wikipedia.org/wiki/Marble_(toy)

[p. 40] "Save the Planet, Honor the Resistance"
"We foreigners, have only one way to prove to France our gratitude: to be killed."
Dimitri Amilakhvari
http://foreignlegion.info/2022/10/23/lieutenant-colonel-dimitri-amilakvari

[p. 54] "Neowise in Syzygy"
"a period of increasingly polarized social stratification and decreasing egalitarianism"
Adapted from Wikipedia entry: https://en.wikipedia.org/wiki/Ubaid_period

KEN WEISNER attended Oberlin College and the Iowa Writers Workshop before going to University of California, Santa Cruz, for PhD work in literature. He has been teaching writing and literature at De Anza College, Cupertino, California, since the mid-nineties. He is the author of *The Sacred Geometry of Pedestrians* (2002), *Anything on Earth* (2010), and *Cricket to Star* (2019) — all from Hummingbird Press. For many years he edited *Quarry West* through Porter College at UCSC, and he currently edits and advises the national edition of *Red Wheelbarrow* through De Anza College. Weisner's poetry has been widely published in journals and anthologies. His work was featured on the *Poets Against the War* website (2003), in *The Music Lover's Poetry Anthology* (Persea, 2007), and in John Chandler and Wilma Marcus Chandler's Willing Suspension Armchair Theater production of *Lost and Found: The Literature of Fathers and Sons* (May, 2009). Garrison Keillor read Weisner's poem "The Gardener" on *The Writer's Almanac* in August of 2010. His work has appeared most recently in *Catamaran, Caesura, Jung Journal: Culture and Psyche, Nine Mile, Perfume River Poetry Review, Phren-Z, Porter Gulch Review, The Twin Bill, and Xinachtli Journal.*